THE SECRET OF THE SQUIGGLY GREEN BOMBERS

... AND MORE!

BY ANA MARÍA RODRÍGUEZ

Enslow Publishing
101 W. 23rd Street
Suite 240
New York, NY 10011
USA

enslow.com

Acknowledgments
The author expresses her immense gratitude to all the scientists who
have contributed to the Animal Secrets Revealed! series. Their comments and
photos have been invaluable to the creation of these books.

Published in 2018 by Enslow Publishing, LLC.
101 W. 23rd Street, Suite 240, New York, NY 10011

Library of Congress Cataloging-in-Publication Data

Names: Rodríguez, Ana María, 1958- author.
Title: The secret of the squiggly green bombers... and more! / Ana María
Rodríguez.
Description: New York : Enslow Publishing, 2018. | Series: Animal secrets
revealed! | Includes bibliographical references and index. | Audience:
Grades 3 to 6.
Identifiers: LCCN 2017007000 | ISBN 9780766086319 (library bound) | ISBN
9780766088498 (paperback) | ISBN 9780766088436 (6-pack)
Subjects: LCSH: Marine animals--Juvenile literature. | Reptiles--Juvenile
literature. | Animal behavior--Research--Juvenile literature.
Classification: LCC QL122.2 .R637 2017 | DDC 591.77--dc23
LC record available at https://lccn.loc.gov/2017007000

To Our Readers: We have done our best to make sure all websites in this book were
active and appropriate when we went to press. However, the author and the publisher
have no control over and assume no liability for the material available on those websites or
on any websites they may link to. Any comments or suggestions can be sent by email to
customerservice@enslow.com.

Photo Credits: Cover, pp. 3 (top left), 7 © 2012 Karen J. Osborne/Smithsonian; pp. 3 (top
right), 12, 13, 16 NOAA Fisheries/Southwest Fisheries Science Center; pp. 3 (center left), 23,
25 Andrea Suria; pp. 3 (bottom right), 28, 29, 31 © Tjkphotography/Dreamstime.com; pp.
3 (bottom left), 35 © Boaz Yunior Wibowo/Dreamstime.com; pp. 6, 9 NOAA; p. 15 Liana
Heberer/NOAA Fisheries/Southwest Fisheries Science Center; pp. 20, 22 Sarah McAnulty;
p. 34 © Dean Bertoncelj/Dreamstime.com; p. 36 Bryan Fry.

★ CONTENTS ★

★

ENTER THE WORLD OF ANIMAL SECRETS

In this volume of Animal Secrets Revealed!, you will tag along with scientists and discover intriguing adaptations that help animals survive in their environments. First, dive into the deep, cold, pitch-black waters of the Pacific Ocean to discover tiny squiggly worms that have an unusual "glowing" strategy to escape hungry predators. Next, take a ride on a fishing boat with biologists who are looking for the hottest fish in the sea. In Hawaii, you will join scientists exploring what squid moms pass long to their eggs to help the eggs survive, even after mom is gone. Then, at a crocodile farm in France, tag along with brave scientists who dared to get close enough to crocodile nests to test the eggs' hatching calls. Finally, learn how a Komodo dragon really kills it prey. Welcome to the world of animal secrets!

1
GREEN BOMBS AWAY!

Marine biologist Karen Osborn is on a ship, sitting in a dark room that has an entire wall covered with TV-like monitors. She fixes her eyes on the monitors as she directs an ROV, a remotely operated vehicle, deep into the ocean beneath her.

"Operating the ROV from the ship is like playing a huge video game," Osborn said. "The monitors show my colleagues and me what the different cameras on the ROV see, and that helps the pilot steer the vehicle to the areas I want to explore."[1]

As the ROV descends into the deep, light dwindles. Osborne flips a switch on her console to turn on the large bright lights of the ROV, revealing the deep, dark sea. "The ROV's light lets me see

An ROV is dropped into the sea from a ship.

animals that live deep down in the sea. We can even see transparent creatures we normally would not know about," Osborn said.

Osborn and her team use an ROV to explore the deep oceans off the coast of California. "Every time the ROV goes down, we see many new creatures," she said. "More than half of the animals we see have not been described by scientists. We cannot study them all, so we focus on those we suspect play important roles in their communities."[2]

One of the creatures that has appeared often in Osborn's ROV monitors is a squiggly worm that is a bit shorter than your little finger and about as wide.

"These worms are abundant and relatively large," Osborn said. "These are clues that they are probably important in their communities. For instance, they might be eating many things and providing food for other animals in the food chain of this area. These deep-water worms also caught my attention because they look and behave in ways I had not seen before."

How to Catch Squiggly Deep-Water Worms

The squiggly worms Osborn wanted to collect live about 2.4 miles (3.8 kilometers) below the ocean surface. Such a deep distance is about two and a half times the depth of the Grand Canyon! At this depth, the sea is not only pitch black, but also very cold. In addition, the weight of the seawater above exerts tremendous pressure on the body of any creature venturing

Two green bombers are in close contact. Notice the green bomber on the top has released some of its "bombs."

so deep. So, Osborn sent the ROV, which was built to stand such an extreme environment. With great care, patience, and skill, the team used the ROV to capture the squiggly worms.

The ROV is about the size of a delivery truck. It carries a special canister with doors on either end that slide open "We gently place this canister over the little worm and close both lids, capturing the worm. Then we bring it to the surface, said Osborn."[3]

Naming a New Species? The scientists named the green bomber *Swima bombiviridis*. The name means green bomber that swims very well.

When Osborn and her colleagues studied the squiggly worms up close in the lab, they realized they had a very unusual new species. The worms have a transparent body, no eyes, and a row of fan-shaped paddles made of fine bristles surrounding their body.[4]

"The worms are excellent swimmers," said Osborn. "They can swim backward and forward by using the fan-shaped paddles. When they feel threatened, they escape by swimming backward very quickly."

The scientists were particularly curious about capsule-like structures, little containers that look like pills, attached to the worm's head.

"We also found several of these capsules at the bottom of the collection canisters," Osborn said. "We wondered what was going on with these capsules."

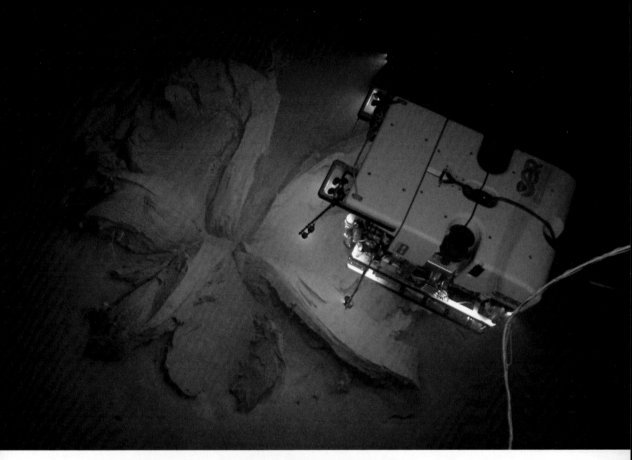

Once deep under the sea, an **ROV** can sample the dark ocean floor and help scientists in their search for new species.

The First Worm Bombardier of the Animal Kingdom

It occurred to the scientists that studying the worms in the dark, the creature's natural habitat, might help them figure out what the capsules do.

"We took the worms to a dark room and carefully poked them, simulating a situation in which the worms might feel threatened," said Osborn. "The worms dropped a capsule or two and swam away. Right away the capsules shone bright green, standing out in the dark room!"[5]

GREEN LIGHT UNDER THE SEA

The bright green light that suddenly shines from the green bomber's capsules is called bioluminescence. This refers to light made by a living organism by means of a chemical reaction. Although bioluminescence is present in some terrestrial animals, it is much more common in aquatic organisms.

The scientists were delighted. They had discovered the first worm bombardier of the animal kingdom. And now the defense secret of the green bomber is out. When a green bomber worm feels threatened, it releases its bombs. The bombs shine bright green, which can distract its predators long enough to give the bomber a chance to escape into the darkness.[6]

2
THIS FISH IS HOT!

icholas Wegner, a marine biologist, is looking at fish gills stored in a jar. The arched-shaped gills belonged to an amazing-looking fish, the opah. Shaped almost like a tire, crimson red with white spots, opah can weigh as much as a ten-year-old boy—about 100 pounds (45 kilograms).

"The opah is not a fish we commonly see during our fishery surveys," Wegner said. "We know very little about them, so when my colleague, biologist Owyn Snodgrass, caught one, he preserved the gills for me to examine."[1]

Wegner studies fish gills, including those of tuna fish and mako sharks. "At first, I was not very interested," Wegner admitted. "I wasn't expecting to find anything unusual. I kept the opah gills in the

Nicholas Wegner holds an opah he caught during one of his research trips.

jar until months later when Snodgrass asked me whether I had looked at them yet."

Wegner got the gills out of the jar that week to dissect; he cut them open to study their insides. "Right away I noticed there were blood vessels inside the gills that were not supposed to be there," Wegner said. "I was curious. I did not know what role the blood vessels were playing in the opah gills, but I had a few ideas. I went with Snodgrass on the next research cruise to learn more about the opah."[2]

Finding Opah

Early in the morning, Wegner and Snodgrass met in a commercial fishing boat they used to survey shark populations. Once on the open ocean, they set a long fishing line with 200 hooks and left it in the water for four hours as part of their survey. When they pulled back the line, they had captured mako and blue sharks as well as an opah.

12

Wegner raised the opah onto the ship using a specially designed stretcher. He tried to place a sensor on the fish to log the temperature of the animal's body. That was easier said than done. The opah, resting on one side in the stretcher half-filled with water, flapped its fin, constantly, splashing water all over Wegner and his colleagues. Only when Snodgrass held the opah's fin still could Wegner finish

Scientists bring an opah into the ship to tag and release.

Nicholas Wegner places a temperature sensor into the pectoral muscles of a captured opah. The sensor simultaneously records both environmental and internal body temperatures after release.

placing the temperature logger. Then, the team slowly and carefully released the opah back into the ocean.[3]

The Tricky Part

The tricky part of the experiment is to get the temperature logger back.

"We use loggers that stay with the fish and record information for various periods of time while the animal goes about its daily activities," Wegner said.

When it finishes recording data, the logger pops up automatically and floats to the surface of the ocean. The logger then transmits a signal that gives the scientists the GPS coordinates they need to find it in the sea.

"Even though we have the GPS coordinates, it is hard to see this little tag floating in the ocean, especially when it is wavy," Wegner said. "It is helpful that the tag gives out a ping once a minute. We can pick up that short, high-frequency signal with sophisticated equipment to try to home in on its location. Hopefully, with each successive signal we get closer and closer until we find the tag. Unfortunately, sometimes we drive right past the tag several times before we find it!"[4]

The Secret of the Opah

When Wegner studied opah closely, he saw that its gills were not the only thing that makes opah different from other fish.

Joe Ludlow poses with his 108.6-pound (49-kg) opah that he caught while fishing near San Diego, California. This fish exceeded the existing opah world record by eighteen pounds.

"I saw that opah have a layer of fatty tissue covering the pectoral or chest muscles," Wegner said. "The fat works like insulation, like a blanket keeping the muscles warm, including the heart. This is something you don't see in other fish."

"Opah also swim differently," said Wegner. "They do not move the body and tail side to side, most other fish. Instead, opah

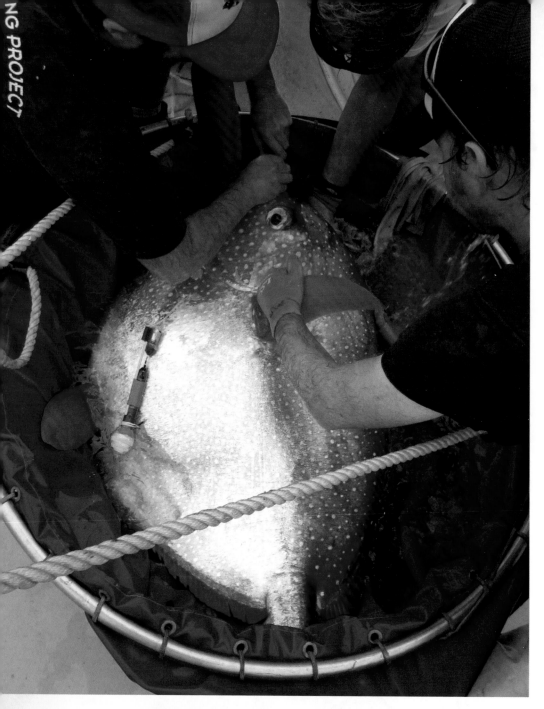

Biologists at **NOAA** Fisheries are preparing an opah for release. Note the temperature data logger placed on the fish's body.

constantly flap their pectoral fins with their large pectoral muscles, similar to a bird flapping its wings. They look almost like penguins swimming. The opah's pectoral muscle is many times larger than the pectoral muscle in most other fish species."[5]

Moreover, all this flapping produces heat that the fatty coat helps keep around the muscles. Being able to keep the heat is useful because fish have a hard time staying warm in cold water. The heat warms the blood rushing toward the gills, which flows very closely to the cold, oxygen-rich blood coming back to the body from the gills. The network of blood vessels carrying warm blood transfers heat to the cold oxygen-rich blood before it enters the core of the body. This keeps the fish warm. This is an example of a countercurrent heat exchange mechanism.[6] Car manufacturers have borrowed this process from nature; they use the same idea in a radiator to keep a car engine cool.

"Soon, I realized that the opah has a way to stay warm in its cold environment," Wegner said.

Between Warm Blooded and Cold Blooded

"We are used to thinking of animals as warm blooded and cold blooded, but the truth is that there are animals in between," Wegner said. "Some fish warm up some parts of their bodies.

For instance, tuna and some sharks warm certain muscles, and swordfish and marlins warm up their eyes and brain."[7]

The opah, on the other hand, warms up most of its body. Still, it does not warm its body nearly as much as a mammal does. On average, the temperature of the opah's muscles is about 10 degrees Fahrenheit (5 degrees Celsius) above that of the surrounding water.

Being able to keep their bodies several degrees above the temperature of their environment makes a big difference for the fish. "The warm-bodied opah is a high-performance predator that swims faster, reacts more quickly, and sees more sharply than colder fish," said Wegner.

The secret is out! The opah is the first fish found to keep its whole body warmer than its environment. It uses the power of its muscles, fatty insulation, and a network of blood vessels inside its gills to keep its body warm.

3
SQUID MOMS TO THE RESCUE

Spencer Nyholm is wearing a brand-new white lab coat, ready to start a day of work in the lab. A marine biologist, Nyholm walks toward the aquarium to collect a Hawaiian bobtail squid for an experiments.

"Suddenly, one of these golf ball-sized squid jumped out of the tank, right toward me and inked me!" said Nyholm. "It covered my new lab coat and the shirt I was wearing underneath in black ink. No matter how much I washed the lab coat, the ink would never come out completely. I then understood why monks of medieval times would write with squid ink. Their writings would practically last forever! On the bright side, I easily knew which one was my lab coat."[1]

Spencer Nyholm observes a Hawaiian bobtail squid in his laboratory.

Moonlight Invisibility Cloak

Despite the squid's revenge, Nyholm has persevered for many
years studying this little relative of the cuttlefish. He first studied
a light organ that helps the squid escape predators. The squid
is most active at night. As it swims over the sandy beds of the
shallow waters of Hawaiian beaches looking for food, the squid
risks becoming other predators' meal. Interestingly, the squid
has a way of becoming practically invisible to its predators.

The squid has a light organ in its body that can surround the squid with a glow that matches the moonlight. As predators such as fish swim under the squid and look toward the surface hunting for it, they cannot see the squid's shape because the glow around it blends with the moonlight-lit background.[2]

It turns out that the squid itself does not make the light. Millions of bacteria that live in the light organ do. This is another example of bioluminescence, light made by a living organism. These bacteria do not harm the squid; they are partners with it. Each helps the other survive in the hostile marine environment. The bacteria make light that camouflages the squid from predators, and the squid provides a home for the bacteria. This type of relationship in which both partners receive benefits

HAWAIIAN BOBTAIL SQUID

How Hawaiian Bobtail Squid Travel from Hawaii to Connecticut

Nyholm and his colleagues travel to Hawaii twice a year to collect Hawaiian bobtail squid. "The squid are nocturnal, so we go to the beach at night with flashlights, nets, and plastic bags. We wait around the shallow water looking for them on the sandy bottom. It helps that when we shine a light on the squid, it freezes like a deer in headlights. We scoop them out carefully with the net, transfer them into a plastic bag with seawater, and fly them with us to our lab at the University of Connecticut where we breed them in aquaria."[3]

is called symbiosis. Interestingly, Hawaiian bobtail squid have another symbiosis that helps their eggs survive.

Good Squid Moms

Nyholm and his colleagues are also studying the second symbiosis of the Hawaiian bobtail squid, which only squid moms have. The females have an organ, the nidamental gland, in their bodies. Many bacteria live inside this gland, or sac. Scientists know that these bacteria do not make the squid sick. The squid mixes the bacteria with the jelly that coats the eggs, lays the eggs in coral rubble, and then leaves.[4]

This Hawaiian bobtail squid is one that Spencer Nyholm studies in his lab.

Nyholm was intrigued. What role could these bacteria play in regard to the eggs?

Cephalopods, such as squid and cuttlefish, seem to be the only animals that have an organ containing bacteria with which to coat their eggs. Other aquatic animals called "brooders," such as lobster and shrimp, do not have such an organ to store these bacteria. Instead, they collect bacteria from their environment and use it to coat the eggs that they carry.

A jelly coat protects the tiny eggs of the Hawaiian bobtail squid. The jelly also keeps the eggs together.

Aquatic animals live in a place that is also home to millions of different kinds of bacteria, as well as fungi, microscopic algae, and zooplankton. Some of these bacteria do not harm other animals, but others are "foulers," as Nyholm calls them. Foulers grow on organisms, such as living eggs, and smother or suffocate them—they stop oxygen from reaching them and the eggs die. Other microbes in the ocean, on the other hand, are useful to the environment because as they grow on dead animals and plants, they recycle the remains. This makes microbes an essential part of the life cycle.

For a squid mom, foulers are bad news. If left alone to do their business of growing on other animals, foulers will suffocate her eggs and her squid babies will never hatch.

"If you are an animal that lays its eggs in water, you need a means to protect them from the foulers that will kill the eggs," Nyholm said.

It might seem odd that squid and other animals would cover their eggs with microbes and then lay them in an environment that is teaming with even more microbes. But it is not odd at all. While many of the microbes in the environment will immediately feed on the eggs, Nyholm suspected that the microbes in the squid jelly that coats the eggs are "good" microbes. They do not eat the eggs; they somehow protect them from being eaten by the "bad" microbes.[5]

To find out whether the bacteria in squid eggs were of the "good" kind, Nyholm and his colleagues collected these bacteria from squid eggs, grew them in the lab, and looked for chemical weapons.

Chemical Weapons

"My colleagues and I had the hypothesis that if the bacteria in squid jelly protect the eggs from the attacks by

> **Foulers Are Everywhere**
> **Animals that lay their eggs on land, such as insects, have the same problem with foulers that aquatic animals have. Billions of hungry microbes will also smother and kill their eggs.**

The researchers found that bacteria in the squid jelly acted like chemical weapons.

fouling organisms, then these "good" bacteria will be able to make chemicals that would stop the "bad" bacteria from growing on the eggs," Nyholm said.

Nyholm and his colleagues knew that this kind of chemical warfare existed between bacteria. Just as much larger organisms do, bacteria compete with each other for food and space. So, the scientists took samples of the jelly and studied the type of bacteria that live in it and the chemicals they make.

They discovered that the bacteria that live in the squid jelly are of a number of different types. One type of these bacteria is blue, which comes from a blue-colored chemical called indigoidine.[6]

Nyholm and his colleagues discovered that indigoidine can effectively stop other bacteria, but not the "good" bacteria, from growing. Specifically, this "chemical weapon" can stop vibrios, a type of fouler bacteria common in seawater that can also cause disease.

"In addition, we found that the bacteria in the jelly can potentially make more than one chemical that can stop 'bad' bacteria," said Nyholm.[7]

The secret is out! Hawaiian bobtail squid moms take good care of their eggs. They coat them with a jelly teaming with bacteria that make "chemical weapons" that can stop "bad" bacteria from killing the eggs. In this way, squid moms give baby squid a better chance to hatch.

4
CROCODILE EGG TIMER

ANile crocodile mom has not wandered far from the same sandy spot for about ninety days. She has snarled at and promptly chased away any unexpected visitors that has dared come near. The reason for her aggressive guarding behavior is soon clear when mom begins to dig, and fifty to sixty newly-hatched baby crocodiles emerge from the underground nest.

At the sight of her babies, mom drops her aggressive behavior and becomes a gentle parent. She carefully carries her babies into her mouth and carries them to the nearby river. She will care for them until they are ready to manage on their own.

As scientists observed the guarding behavior of these crocodiles, they soon noticed that

Three baby crocodiles hatch in sync, a strategy that helps them survive in their hostile environment.

baby crocodiles inside the eggs underground raise a racket of calls shortly before hatching. Many researchers thought that the sounds from some of the eggs triggered hatching in the other eggs in the nest, like a call to emerge all together. The calls also seemed to prompt mom to open the nest. No scientist, however, had carried out experiments to test these observations. Amélei Vergne and Nicolas Mathevon decided to take the challenge.[1]

What Baby Crocs Do

Vergne and Mathevon went to La Ferme aux Crocodiles (Crocodile Farm), a zoo in France. They took with them

28

recordings of crocodile pre-hatching calls they had made. Would playing the recorded calls to crocodile eggs would trigger the eggs to hatch?

In a first set of experiments, the scientists collected seventeen crocodile eggs from the zoo. All the eggs were near the time of hatching, about ten days away. Then, Vergne and Mathevon played the recordings to some of the crocodile eggs and observed the behavior of the babies inside the eggs during the following ten minutes. To other eggs, the

Mom alligator carefully carries one of her babies in her mouth. No creature would dare bother that baby alligator.

NILE CROCODILE

The Nile crocodile lives in sub-Saharan Africa. Scientists think that this crocodile is the second largest living reptile in the world, after the saltwater crocodile.

scientists played random noise, and to others they played no sound at all.[2]

The scientists found that eight of the ten crocodile eggs that heard recorded pre-hatching calls answered the calls, and about half of them hatched within ten minutes of hearing the playbacks. On the other hand, the eggs that heard either noise or no sound remained mostly quiet and only one hatched after hearing the calls.

What Mom Crocodiles Do

In a second set of experiments, Vergne and Mathevon had to figure out how to test the pre-hatching calls on crocodile moms guarding a nest. Would moms begin digging, opening the nest if they heard the recordings?[3]

At La Ferme aux Crocodiles, the keepers usually remove the eggs from crocodile nests a few days after mom lays them, and they care for them. Despite having an eggless nest, crocodile moms continue guarding the nest. This situation helped Vergne and Mathevon do their experiment.

To test how crocodile moms responded to the recorded calls, the scientists first drove mom away from the nest, and, while she was distracted, they placed a loudspeaker underground on the eggless nest. They did not have much time to

A Nile crocodile mom digs her eggs into the sand. She will guard the nest until she hears the hatching calls that cue her to dig the nest open.

do this. Most crocodile moms were back on the nest within five minutes![4]

The scientists then played the pre-hatching recordings, random noise, or no sound, and observed what the moms did. As Vergne and Mathevon had anticipated, crocodile moms paid attention more often and more quickly to the recorded calls than to random noise or no noise. Eight of the ten moms began digging when they heard the calls. Only one opened the nest when she heard the noise.

> **Science Tongue Twister**
> **The scientific name of the Nile crocodile is *Crocodylus niloticus*.**

The secret is out! Unborn crocodiles produce calls that trigger the eggs in an underground nest to hatch at about the same time. The calls also cue crocodile moms to dig the eggs out.[5]

Vergne and Mathevon think that having a call that synchronizes hatching and recruits mom's help in the process gives newborn crocodiles a head start in life.[6] Baby crocodiles are easy prey, so hatching in sync and having mom's help most certainly increases their chances of survival.

5
HOW KOMODO DRAGONS KILL THEIR PREY

It's a hot day and Bryan Fry, reptile biologist, is in the field observing the world's largest lizard on the hunt. From a distance, he sees a magnificent looking Komodo dragon lying still on the ground, alert, waiting. It quickly thrusts its split tongue in and out to smell its surroundings.

"Komodo dragons are solitary, intelligent hunters," Fry said. "They anticipate their prey's movements and plan their attacks accordingly. First, a Komodo dragon observes that deer or pigs come repeatedly down a certain path at a certain time of the day. Then, on its next hunt, the Komodo dragon gets into a position from which it can see its prey crossing their usual paths at their usual time."[1]

The attack comes quickly. The fast Komodo dragon rushes forward, thrusting its forked tongue in and out,
thrashing its tail. It bites and kills its prey.

"Komodo dragons have a successful hunt nearly nine
out of ten attempts," Fry said. "That's higher than the hunting

**This Komodo dragon is eating prey that is small enough to
swallow whole.**

Komodo dragons open their mouths wide to grab prey, and they pull with their strong neck muscles.

success of most other predators. It makes the Komodo dragon a super predator."

Grip and Rip

Fry and his colleagues have studied in detail what makes Komodo dragons super predators. First, the scientists looked at the animal's skull, jaws, and teeth and compared them with those of other top predators, such as the Australian saltwater crocodile.[2]

Bryan Fry poses with Monty, a captive Komodo dragon.

The scientists took images of the skulls with a medical scanner and created 3D images. They then used these images in computer models to simulate what would happen to the bones if they applied different forces at different angles.

The results revealed that the power of the bite of Komodo dragons is weaker than that of the Australian saltwater crocodile. However, the dragon's skull can take strong pulling forces.[3]

"These results match what we see in the field," Fry said. "Komodo dragons might not crush their prey with a bite as strong as that of some crocodiles, but they are very strong when it comes to gripping their prey. For instance, they can hold on to a large pig while pulling on it, and they don't let it go easily when the prey pulls back, trying to escape."[4]

The dragon's teeth work hand in hand with the powerful grip of the jaws, providing ripping power that helps kill the prey quickly. Fry and his colleagues looked at the Komodo dragon's teeth under the electron microscope. The teeth are sharp and have jagged or serrated edges on the cutting side.[5] This makes it easier for the Komodo dragon to rip the flesh of their prey. Deep cuts usually make the animal bleed until it passes out and dies. Interestingly, that is not all the dragon has that makes it a super predator.

Venom in Its Mouth

Komodo dragons are members of the family of poisonous or venomous monitor lizards. "In previous studies, my colleagues and I had discovered that there are more venomous monitor lizards than we thought there were," Fry said. "Then, I thought about the dragons. Could they be using venom to hunt? I realized then that I had to study this magnificent lizard!"

For Fry, studying Komodo dragons, the largest lizard alive, was his childhood dream come true. "I was thrilled to study Komodo dragons because I had been drawn toward these

KOMODO DRAGON'S HABITAT

Caring for the Komodo Dragon's Habitat

Komodo dragons are a vulnerable species; they are at risk of becoming endangered. Although they are protected, their habitats are getting smaller and smaller. This can lead to the dragon's extinction. Protecting the dragons might be in people's best interest. Fry and other scientists think that some of the poisons the dragon uses to kill prey might one day be the source of new medicines that can save the lives of people with heart disease and other conditions. Saving the dragons could one day save people.

amazing animals since I was a child," Fry said. "For me, studying the dragons is like a shark biologist studying great white sharks. It doesn't get better than that!"[6]

To study whether Komodo dragons are poisonous, Fry and his colleagues took a trip to the zoo. With a medical scanner, they took images of the inside of the mouth of Komodo dragons. They found a venom gland inside the mouth, stretching along the jaws, lining up with the teeth.[7]

Komodo dragons are very dangerous animals, but those that live in zoos become less aggressive and easier to work with than those in the wild. This helped Fry, especially when he decided to take venom samples from the glands in the teeth-studded mouth of live dragons.

"With the help of the zookeepers who take care of the dragons, we restrained a very well-behaved captive animal," Fry said. "Then, I ran my finger along the inside of the animal's jaw, slightly pressing from the back to the front of the gland. When I did that, venom oozed between the teeth and I collected it."[8]

The analysis of the venom revealed that it contains a number of compounds. Interestingly, some of them can quickly lower blood pressure, cause massive bleeding, prevent clotting, and induce shock in prey.

"Some of the compounds in Komodo venom work just like those in snake venom," said Fry.

Grip, Rip, and Drip

When Fry and his colleagues put all the laboratory clues together with their observations from the field, they had a much better picture of how Komodo dragons kill their prey. The dragons grip, rip, and drip.

When Komodo dragons bite their prey, they grip and pull back with great strength. Then, the sharp, serrated teeth rip deep wounds on the flesh, which allows the venom to drip into the wounds. The powerful poisons stop the blood from clotting. The animal cannot stop bleeding, which leads to shock and death.

> **Science Tongue Twister**
> **The scientific name of the Komodo dragon is *Varanus komodoensis*.**

Some scientists, however, were not convinced that the dragons use venom to kill their prey. They argued that, instead,

Komodo dragons use bacteria to put down prey. They proposed that when the dragons bite prey, bacteria in their mouths enter the wounds and cause an infection that kills the animal.[9]

When Fry and his colleagues looked for the experimental evidence supporting this hypothesis, they found none. The idea that Komodo dragons use bacteria to kill prey had come from observations in the late 1960s of large prey injured by the dragons, such as water buffaloes, developing fatal infections. In time, this idea became popular.

To clear the myth, Fry teamed up with Ellie Goldstein, an expert in the microbes in human and animal bite wounds. Together they looked at the type of bacteria living in the mouths of Komodo dragons.

"Komodo dragons have no deadly bacteria in their mouths," Fry said. "Actually, they have fewer bacteria in their mouths than other hunters, such as lions or Tasmanian devils," said Fry. "Komodos are actually remarkably clean animals."[10]

The secret is out! Komodo dragons use their strong grip to rip deep wounds open with their sharp, serrated teeth and drip poisons that quickly cause their prey to bleed to death.

HANDS-ON ACTIVITY:

Heat Exchange for Breakfast

The opah is not the only one that uses a mechanism of heat exchange in its daily life. People do, too. The air conditioning equipment in your home, the refrigerator, and cars use the same principle of physics to keep your home, your food, and the car cool.

Here you will carry out an experiment that will demonstrate that the principle of heat exchange can help you solve a problem: your breakfast is too hot to eat. If you wait for it to cool down on its own, you might be late for school! Ask for help from an adult when using the microwave.

What you need

- ★ 2 breakfast bowls
- ★ 1.5 cups of oatmeal cereal ("Old fashioned" style that needs two minutes to cook)
- ★ 2 cups of milk or water
- ★ microwave
- ★ spoon
- ★ 1 cup frozen blueberries; keep them in the freezer until you reach step 6, below
- ★ kitchen gloves for holding hot items
- ★ kitchen thermometer
- ★ timer

What to do
1. Mix one cup of milk or water with 3/4 cup of oatmeal in each of the bowls.
2. Heat each bowl in the microwave for two minutes.
3. Ask an adult for help removing the hot bowls from the microwave.
4. Slowly mix the content in the bowls with the spoon. Start the timer.
5. Measure the temperature of each cereal mix.
6. Add the frozen berries to one of the bowls; mix gently with the spoon.
7. Measure the temperature of each bowl 1 minute, 5 minutes, and 10 minutes later. Write the results in the table below.

Bowl	Temp. at time 0 (°F)	Temp. at 1 min. (°F)	Temp. at 5 min. (°F)	Temp. at 10 min. (°F)
Without berries				
With berries				

Results
1. How long did it take each bowl to cool down enough for you to eat it?
2. Explain how the frozen berries in your hot cereal help you save time in the morning.

★ CHAPTER NOTES ★

Chapter 1: Green Bombs Away!

1. Dr. Karen Osborn, phone interview with the author, December 12, 2016.
2. Ibid.
3. Ibid.
4. Karen J. Osborn, Steven Haddock, Fredrik Pleijel, Laurence Madin, and Greg Rouse, "Deep-Sea, Swimming Worms with Luminescent "Bombs," *Science*, vol. 325, 2009, p. 964.
5. Dr. Osborn.
6. Osborn et al.

Chapter 2: This Fish Is Hot!

1. Dr. Nicholas Wegner, Skype interview with the author, December 4, 2016.
2. Ibid.
3. Ibid.
4. Ibid.
5. Ibid.
6. Nicholas C. Wegner, Owyn Snodgrass, Heidi Dewar, and John Hyde, "Whole-Body Endothermy in a Mesopelagic Fish, the Opah, *Lampris guttatus*," *Science*, vol.348, 2015, p. 786.
7. Ibid.

Chapter 3: Squid Moms to the Rescue

1. Dr. Spencer Nyholm, Skype interview with the author, December 4, 2016.
2. Ibid.
3. Ibid.
4. Andrew Collins, Matthew Fullmer, Johann Gogarten and Spencer Nyholm, "Comparative Genomics of *Roseobacter* Clade Bacteria

Isolated from the Accessory Nidamental Gland of *Euprymna scolopes*," *Frontiers in Microbiology*, 2015, http://dx.doi.org/10.3389/fmicb.2015.00123.

5. Ibid.

6. Samantha Gromek, Andrea Suria, Matthew Fullmer, Jillian García, Johann Peter Gogarten, Spencer Nyholm, and Marcy Balunas, "Leisingera sp. JC1, a Bacterial Isolate from Hawaiian Bobtail Squid Eggs, Produces Indigoidine and Differentially Inhibits Vibrios," Frontiers in Microbiology, 2016, https://doi.org/10.3389/fmicb.2016.01342.

7. Ibid.

Chapter 4: Crocodile Egg Timer

1. Amélie Vergne and Nicolas Mathevon, "Crocodile Egg Sounds Signal Hatching Time," *Current Biology*, vol. 18, 2008, p. R513.

2. Ed Yong, "Crocodiles signal hatching time by calling from inside their eggs," *Not Exactly Rocket Science—A Blog, National Geographic*, June 25, 2008, http://phenomena.nationalgeographic.com/2008/06/25/crocodiles-signal-hatching-time-by-calling-from-inside-their-eggs/.

3. Vergne and Mathevon.

4. Ibid.

5. Ibid.

6. Yong.

Chapter 5: How Komodo Dragons Kill Their Prey

1. Dr. Bryan Fry, Skype interview with the author, January 5, 2017.

2. Bryan Fry, et al., "A Central Role for Venom in Predation by *Varanus komodoensis* (Komodo Dragon) and the Extinct Giant *Varanus (Megalania) priscus*" *Proceedings of the National Academy of Sciences*, vol. 106, 2009, p. 8969.

3. Ibid.

4. Dr. Fry.

5. Fry et al.

6. Dr. Fry.

7. Fry et al.

8. Dr. Fry.

9. Ellie Goldstein, Kerin Tyrrell, Diane Citron, Cathleen Cox, Ian Recchio, Ben Okimoto, Judith Bryja, and Bryan Fry, "Anaerobic and Aerobic Bacteriology of the Saliva and Gingiva from 16 Captive Komodo Dragons (*Varanus komodoensis*): New Implications for the "Bacteria as Venom" Model," *Journal of Zoo and Wildlife Medicine*, vol. 44, 2013, p. 262.

10. Ibid.

★ GLOSSARY ★

bacteria ★ A type of microscopic organism; some can cause disease, but most of them do not.

bioluminescence ★ The production of light by a living organism by means of a chemical reaction.

blood vessel ★ A structure shaped like a tube that carries blood to all parts of the body.

capsule ★ A container, usually shaped like a cylinder.

electron microscope ★ A microscope that uses beams of electrons instead of light to make small objects look bigger.

gill ★ A breathing organ of a fish that allows oxygen dissolved in water to pass into the organism.

gland ★ An organ in the body that makes substances the body needs.

habitat ★ The natural environment in which plants or animals live.

hatch ★ To come out of an egg.

indigoidine ★ A blue compound produce by some bacteria to stop other bacteria from growing.

predator ★ An animal that hunts other animals.

prey ★ An animal hunted by other animals.

ROV ★ Remotely-operated vehicle used in deep sea exploration.

symbiosis ★ A relationship between two organisms that benefits both.

terrestrial ★ Having to do with land.

venom ★ Poison.

★ FURTHER READING ★

Books

Bell, Samantha. *Cuttlefish*. North Mankato MN: Cherry Lake Publishing, 2014.

DK Smithsonian. *Ocean: A Visual Encyclopedia*. New York, NY: DK Children, 2015.

Marsh, Laura. *Alligators and Crocodiles*. Des Moines, IA: National Geographic Children's Books, 2015.

Somervill, Barbara. *Monitor Lizard*. North Mankato MN: Cherry Lake Publishing, 2014.

Websites

National Geographic Kids

kids.nationalgeographic.com/animals/nile-crocodile/#croco-dile-teeth.png
Learn more about the Nile crocodile.

National Oceanic and Atmospheric Administration

games.noaa.gov
Explore many different games that teach you more about oceans and Earth's atmosphere.

★ INDEX ★